DIVERSIFLY

Poetry and Art
on
Britain's Urban Birds

Edited by Nadia Kingsley

Fair Acre Press

Published by Fair Acre Press in 2018

www.fairacrepress.co.uk

Edited by Nadia Kingsley

Copyright of poems and images rests with the authors and artists cited in the index pages: Pages 102 - 104 which constitute an extension of this copyright page.

All rights reserved. No part of this publication may be reproduced, stored in a retrieval system or transmitted, in any form or by any means without the prior permission of the publisher, nor be otherwise circulated in any form of binding or cover other than that in which it is published and without a similiar condition being imposed on the subsequent purchaser.

Typeset in Georgia and Garamond by Nadia Kingsley
Internal design by Nadia Kingsley

Printed and bound by Lightning Source

Lightning Source has received Chain of Custody (CoC) certification from:
The Forest Stewardship Council™ (FSC®)
Programme for the Endorsement of Forest Certification™ (PEFC™)
The Sustainable Forestry Initiative® (SFI®)

A CIP catalogue record for this title is available from the British Library.

ISBN 978-1-911048-26-8

Title Page Image by Eileen Schaer

Front Cover Jay Image by ATM (ATMstreetart)
Back Cover Chaffinch Image by ATM (ATMstreetart)

The Cover's Birds' silhouettes & Vector graphic designs by Freepik, Creativepack/ Freepik, Sketchepedia/ Freepik and kjpargeter/ Freepik.

Cover Design by Algimantas Murza

Sparrowhawk in Belfast, Adele Pound

Introduction

This book grew out of the close encounters I have had with birds when visiting central London from my home on the Shropshire-Wales border. I noticed how much closer I could get to blackbirds and other shy birds there. I noticed the number of people with headphones to their ears, and phones in front of their eyes. I thought about the joy I get from watching birds and how at my lowest times their constancy, their flight and their song have enlivened me.

You will see from the contents page that only a sample of birds seen in Britain's towns and cities are included, and that there are a particularly large number of responses to both pigeons and gulls. I like this. These are the birds the poets and artists who took part in this project responded to. I have chosen work I hope you will enjoy – whether you are an expert or novice in poetry, art, or ornithology.

At www.fairacrepress.co.uk you can read the blogs I wrote on urban birds to encourage people to pick up a pen or paintbrush. There you can also download or stream six free podcasts: conversations and readings featuring my favourite UK nature poets: Alison Brackenbury, Gillian Clarke, Chris Kinsey, David Morley, Katrina Porteous and Richard Osmond. You can also join naturalist Brett Westwood and myself on an urban bird walk podcast in Stourbridge, West Midlands.

I would particularly like to thank the poets I commissioned to write a bird poem who are not known for, or used to, writing about nature: Brian Bilston, Carrie Etter, Andrew McMillan, Sabrina Mahfouz, Kaite O'Reilly, Emma Purshouse, Amaal Said, James Sheard and Dorothea Smartt. And my sincere thanks go to Arts Council England.

Nadia Kingsley

Contents

Foreword by Brett Westwood	6 - 7
Barn Owl	9
Blackbird	10 - 13
Blue Tit	14
Crow	15 - 17
Duck	18
Goldfinch	19
Goose	20 - 21
Heron	22
Jackdaw	23
Long-tailed Tit	24 - 25
Magpie	26 - 30
Mistle Thrush	31
Moorhen	32
Peregrine Falcon	33
Pigeon	34 - 45
Red Kite	46 - 47
Robin	48 - 51
Rook	52 - 53
Seagull	54 - 61
Sparrow	62 - 63
Starling	64 - 67
Swallow	68 - 70
Swan	71
Swift	72 - 73
Thrush	74 - 75
Wagtail	76 - 77
Woodpecker	78
Woodpigeon	79
Wren	80
Birds in general	81 - 91
Biographies	92 - 101
Index	102 - 103

Hooded Crows in Belfast, Adele Pound

Foreword

Tuning In

Wildlife-watchers can seem a breed apart, apparently blessed with a sixth sense for detecting their quarry and an ability, unavailable to mere mortals, to conjure the unexpected.

An example: I've lost count of the people who've told me of their inability to find a kingfisher – the sorrowful implication being that if they can't locate the most dazzling of British birds – then what hope have they in seeing less spectacular species?

Luckily, there is a knack to kingfisher spotting. The secret is to listen for the sharp "chik-ee" call, then look in its direction just above the water surface and you should see the bird flying arrow-straight; so bright that it's pursued by an aquamarine afterglow.

Get the knack and a new world of birds will reveal itself. I think of it as tuning in. Learn what to look and listen for – and a stroll around your local park or a walk to the corner shop will uncover a hitherto hidden world of new neighbours, each with its own timetable. It all comes with practice, but keep at it, and your knowledge will grow:

Step outside on a cloudy November night and hear pinpricks of sound piercing the skies. Our superstitious ancestors interpreted these as the cries of airborne witches, bent on malefaction. We know now that they are the piercing calls of migrating redwings – and that these rusty-flanked, Scandinavian thrushes are "shouting" to keep contact with each other, as they fly by night between their breeding and wintering grounds.

At any time of year and anywhere there are trees, keep your ears cocked for the sharp "chik" call of a great spotted woodpecker, a bird which is more common than you might think. Its dumpy silhouetted shape bounding laboriously away is instantly identifiable even when you're denied its glorious chequered plumage; or look to the very tops of trees, where they often perch – tummies pressed against the uppermost twigs.

And it isn't all about sound.

Look upwards: and you might see a buzzard planing overhead through a lattice of branches or a treecreeper inching its way along its arboreal thoroughfare.

In spring there's that special thrill which only the returning swifts, dark anchors among scudding clouds, can bring. It can be hard to find seasonal connections, now more of us are city dwellers – but swifts are universal – scything over town and country bringing us a taste of tropical Africa for a few precious months. They remind us that tuning in to the seasons brings its own delicious experiences.

The more you observe and explore, the more intriguing your neighbourhood becomes: the blackbirds stabbing worms on the winter grass may have travelled from Scandinavia; the black-headed gulls squabbling for the handfuls of birdseed around the park lake could have raised their chicks last summer on a Lithuanian shore; and don't assume that the mallards jostling for the same bounty are all home grown – some may be wild ducks from Continental Europe.

Much of our wildlife face challenging times. Many familiar birds, including house sparrows and swifts, are in decline.

But it's not all bad news.

Last March, in my tiny town centre garden, I was astonished to see a buzzard plundering frogspawn from a pond that is smaller than a bath. Peregrines occasionally dash over my house and even ravens are regular now, cronking sonorously as they power overhead on anthracite wings.

As a teenager getting to grips with birdwatching, I associated peregrines with Welsh hills and Cornish cliffs. I still need to pinch myself to believe it's really happening here in the West Midlands.

But it is, and birds are a constant source of wonder. This same sense of wonder has been captured, so expertly, by the poets and artists in this book. Enjoy!

Brett Westwood
January 2018

Katrinka Wilson

Lord Street

It was Saturday, the morning of my wedding.
The Barn Owl was coming for me from a distance,
flying mad, and maddened by the light. It took

the long arcade of Lord Street, racing straight
beneath the rooflights, ticking past
the iron pillars with their twists and curlicues.

And the women ducked their hair away
from its talons, men batted at it stupidly,
some ducked into the doorways – of the hat shop,

the cake shop, the shoe shop, the beautician's.
The owl held its head, its heart-shape, dead still
but there was little grace in its flight, ragged,

feathery, beating against the sloping sun.
It stared at something hollow in me, unblinking
and yet lost; chaotic, yet compelled to stare,

each of us, into the pool of ourselves.
At the last second, it veered away. I did not.

James Sheard

Chorus

Soon,

The City's silence
 will be broken.
And a day born.

When a blackbird sings,
From a high perch;
And announces dawn.

David Rudd-Mitchell

Nadia Kingsley

Dora Williams

Blackbird

He stands stone-still
on his song-post
to deliver his song,

and with each short phrase,
old familiar melodies
tell us he's alive.

He's a dark star
who thinks he doesn't belong
in this place sometimes,

but proclamations
from his secret woodland past
cover all England

and the high pitched trills
of his rich powerful voice
brush against our skin,

and he's here with us
helping so many voices
deliver our song.

Mary Matusz

Deborah Vass

Nesting

That day was one
for sorrow.
Your nest was carefully concealed,
deep in dense honeysuckle bower.
I never knew you were there.
But the magpies did.
They'd been watching you.
Their beady eyes noting
your frequent visits,
to and fro.

They took your young.
Every single one.
Your shed roof requiem,
a simple service
delivered to a twilight congregation,
shared your grief.

We try to defend our nests,
protect our loved ones
from those, that trespass
against us.
Sometimes
we fail.
That day was one
for sorrow.

Jen Hawkins

Deborah Vass

Mark Mennell

Blue Tit

I heard the small, feathered thud this time,
crack of a thimble-skull striking
the freshly streak-free back-door glass.

Limp as a mitten, a perfect dab
in blue-grey and nursery-wall yellow.
I knelt on the lino at the threshold,

scooped him up, calibrated my grip,
the thrumming skitter of his heartbeat
visible at the whitish divot in his breast-down.

I knelt, thought about collisions,
how the spirit flies clean out of the body
to escape the violence of impact,

how humans may live on in shock,
less than half-tethered to their hearts, or else
die like animals, not able to make it back.

His eyes came and went, inkdrops
scrying a slow drowning, the bird in him
sinking and surfacing, all the while

I knelt in fear of losing him, losing him
for nothing, for only our house standing
complacent in his flightpath.

I tapped to remind his crown about the sky,
blew faithfully across his struggling face –
in a blurred instant, he was gone.

Kirsten Luckins

Crow Journey

I watch from the bus
unruly upstarts, black slicksters
swaggering quick footed,
skippety hop, they bounce drop
to the only green turfed strip;
a murder on the wing.

They bring the gang
to smash and grab,
squabble, squawk,
chase off sparrow, hawk
and strike with beaks of black
shellac defending short lived turf.

Delinquent urban thieves
these 'Jets' with their bravura
of cackle speak & stolen swag
in every beak & cockeyed pose
full of guile, a rose- eyed wink
that makes me smile.

The city skyline is filled
with ragged bickering,
their language,
mine, mine, mine.

Tina Cole

Sue Spawn

Heather Fowler

Corvus

You plunge, sudden as rejection,
onto the street outside the library
where pushchairs flock and young mothers huddle
under the broad wings of its porch.

You're a squawk of anarchy
among the ordered tubs of town council flowers;
what you're thought to augur no petunia-packed container
can contain.
                Sparrows   scatter.
Begonias shrink
        and slink away.
A phone ringtones a warning.

You eye the rim of a bin brimful
of burger wrappings
but you're newly-fledged,
and flight's a foreign language,
so you utter a guttural *kraah* from the edge
of the kerb instead.
Your voice is Viking and your actions match –
kebabbing moss then tossing   it   away,
beaking weeds from pavement cracks,
raiding the gutter-clutter
      of fag butts and leaves –
till, bored, you stalk to a low wall,
          flexflail   stretchflap   hop
and   somehow
              you're airborne
up up   then quicksprawl
    onto the roof
             of a bus stop.

Another, your mother perhaps, lands
with more grace – straightaway your bill's agape,
yet otherwise, you're all restraint: with her, nun-humble.
Her caw's a smoker's cough that coaxes you
    to follow as she flies off,
and though you don't manage to soar,

you still   rise   high   above pubtalk, knotted
    streets, concrete misbeliefs, centuries
of dark-plumed superstition.

Susan Richardson

Some things can be relied on

I have a friend, who
without a child to his name
still visits the ducks
at West Park, Wolverhampton.

He talks to the man who works there, says:
The parakeets have recently
breached 'Duck Island'
after years of attempts
by the other birds, who cherish their homes
from heron to wren,
to keep them off it.

Don't expect, *he added,*
to see any of those
'little brown jobbies'
fledge from there, come the next Spring.

A sad thing to happen
them coming up from London,
but at least, *I say,* the ducks still remain
all varied in their combinations
all quacking as they fly or swim
so cheerily, through
this beleaguered city.

Nadia Kingsley

Ann Bridges

Adele Pound

Goldfinches
for Jane

Finally it's warm and gardens again
flower. Walking out beyond the harbour
and new railings already salt-rusted

I remember a February wind
and a winterbrown buddleia trickling
small birds which I had to stop and admire

although only later I could name them
goldfinch. I watched as one by one they took
flight till like a 'Low Battery' warning

the last one trilled and followed the rest to
wherever they next assembled and I'm left
with the afternoon open before me.

Ken Cockburn

"If Canada Geese were human they would be lounging around all day doing nothing, claiming every welfare benefit in the book...."

Robert Hardman, Daily Mail Columnist

Specular on the Wolverhampton 21

The cold grips them in its beak
a displaced flock – Branta Canadensis.
Camped for winter
tottering together on their turned in toes
wind shivering their feathers.
Sieving grey puddles
ankle deep in mire
intent on survival.
Close by
on the humming ring road
are a monotony of traffic lights –
the only things that ever seem to change.

The only things that ever seem to change
are a monotony of traffic lights
on the humming ring road.
Close by
intent on survival
ankle deep in mire
sieving grey puddles
wind shivering their feathers
tottering together on their turned in toes
camped for winter
a displaced flock – Homo sapiens.
The cold grips them in its beak.

Emma Purshouse

Giancarlo Facchinetti

Heron

He's as unexpected
as royalty

on this river-less estate.
A rook sees him off

and I'm at a loss
to describe his going;

something about
a bike in the sky,

a ghost in an unbuttoned raincoat
late for a train.

Roy Marshall

Gordon Yapp

Adele Pound

March 21st

Two black jackdaws
silent silhouettes
elegiac and perfect
sit mutually placed
in a cherry tree.
No blossom yet
only tiny knots of promise
plump and waiting to pop.
Melting snow drips noisily from
an overhead gutter.
A solitary car splashes slowly
down the street.

The town clock
moon-faced and loud
chimes the everlasting hour.
In this moment
no sudden revelations
just the eternal vernal
of equinox ticking clocks
held tight in winter's grasp
struggling to be free from
this snow-cold day
rough patched and frayed
from edge to edge.

Lynden Rees-Roberts

Long-tailed Tits

A grid of names and greyness
has been laid on this land.
In great blank boxes
in Bittern Road and Kestrel Way,
stuff is being made or moved
for money.

Among small pockets of the past,
in old oaks where hedges were,
a band of small adventurers
are pecking a scant living,
somehow, anyhow, from twigs,
keeping in contact
with soft, thin calls,
before launching themselves
over tarmac oceans
to the next unnamed green island.

Mark Totterdell

Gordon Yapp

the long-tailed titmouse (community)

on the outer circle
(part way between the walled garden
and the artery road)
they surprise us.
A small disturbance
above our heads
rosy pellets with long black tails
        zip between branches
disappear.
        We hear their laughter
tsee, tsee they tease
as they gather
and they dart to the next green cover
calling to each other: *see here, over here, go
here* -
        too fast to see their faces
            but here silver on a tail feather
        and here a white streaked head

on our way to work in the garden
we fall in with this community, we gather
and keep company with these most sociable of birds:
tiny acrobats with ruddy breasts,
they travel in parties, search for food together,
play together, build nests together
help to raise each other's young; pitch in.

Andrea Robinson

Paul Kielty

Chattermag in Four Voices

Chattermag, chatterpie, Cornish pheasant,
marget, miggy, madge of gossip, mok-apie,
haggister, pyenate, the maggot of Lincolnshire,
piet, pioden, pioghaid, piannot, pyet, pyat.

1

Every day you spout your glottal language at me,
or rattle like a furious wasp gaoled in a tin.
I seek out your mutinous monologues in trees,
your rat-a-tat-tat consonants
raw and raucous against my ear.
Oh for a vowel to soften all these syllables,
the yearning woo-wooing of an owl.

2

Collecting in your mischief
The platoon falls in for inspection:
'at close interval, dress right, DRESS.'
No standing at ease with your
tch-tch-tch-tch disapproval,
that scornful tongue fabled, if split,
to master human words.

3

Pica-pica bird valued for balance,
the precision of your poised Yin and Yang,
your monochrome plumes predict
delight and harmonious plenty.
Totemic protector warning of the wolf,
you bridge the river of the Milky Way,
messaging joy 鹊

4

Misery guts, maligned minstrel
refusing to sing to the dying Christ.
No note of compassion from your gape,
just mutterings. Malevolent malingerer
hoisting yourself to Noah's roof, preferring
the perils of the flood to paired company,
the buffeting barrage echoing your call

nanpie, ninut, pianate, piannot, pynot, pyot, pyenate,
piet, pioden, pioghaid, piannot, pyet, pyat,
piet, pyat, pyet, pyot, pyenate, pynot
piet, pyat, pyet, pyot

Kaite O'Reilly

Gordon Yapp

The Running Sky
after reading Tim Dee in a Liverpool café

As a boy I fascinated in the sky that sang,
the sky that danced and abandoned itself
to chaos and change.
Lost in a new city
I envied the arrogant strut of the magpie;
black as crowsong
black as the taunt that there was always something,
high above the stone, glass canopy,
somewhere else.

George Aird

Giancarlo Facchinetti

Magpie

Cock of the walk, of the square swept just for him
of studs of gum and plastic wrap.
This here's the city's kingpin. See how he struts,

dapper as Capone in his suit and spats.
Imagine a gun slung underwing, and cigarettes.
Moonshine in a monogrammed flask.

He keeps each gleam and glittering thing. A tax:
foil packets, ear-less pearls with silver backs,
and the double score of shining lid

and cream filched from the newsagent's mat.
And there his club of mobsters, glossy-tuxed,
rattling the statues with their gunfire chat.

I've seen them flatten pigeons in a mood.
I've seen them swagger, cocky, by the cat
who sleeps outside on the chip-shop bins,

dreaming of cod and feathered things
rounding out his old bones to fat. Then: *scat!*
A toddler runs, all whoops and waving arms a-flap,

and the magpies lift in a sheet of black. For a moment,
the whole sky is dark as pitch, and then
they wheel away. And the square is suddenly light, and plain,

like a storm has broken, done with its old havoc.

Cheryl Pearson

And the Dream-Magpie Speaks

This is for the superstitious few
who always triple salute the lone bird
pecking at a poet's squashed roadkill.

This is for the girl of three and the boy of four
who lives up her lane. This is for the joyous two —
they know that seven holds a secret never to be told,

that there are numbers for kisses and for wishes —
who saw screens through black and white eyes
watching the hip flipside, the devil's own bird.

This is for the stealers of gold and silver chains,
who know the edge of dreams lets lost loves
live on. This is for those who don't believe
in dream-magpies or sorrow.

Jill Munro

Dora Williams

Singing Bird

Up somewhere in the foreshortened
row of plane trees, high in their crowns
and singing on a feedback loop –
whee oo whee oo then a carousel
of other notes – the bird sets off
an echo of myself that I can't find.
The sky's a locked-in grey, the air
overwarm and the bird in December
singing not my heart out but
an element impartial, indifferent
which I'm not – the islands within me
are sinking and I'm afraid
that this bird so loud and clear
may be a blow-in unable to
survive in the park or that the song,
not song thrush not blackbird, *whee
oo whee,* in this time of changes
all the greater for being invisible,
is itself undergoing a change.
I could divert under the seedball
pendulums but fear impels me
forward: I leave the song behind.

Fiona Moore

Mistle thrush nest

Suspending disbelief
as we wait on a red light –
five unhinged heads, poised
between top and base heat
of amber,
green.

Jayne Stanton

Deborah Vass

Moorhen

I don't like the word
akimbo
but it's the only way to describe
the legs of the moorhen
who ducked and ran
across the Headcorn road
braving a barrage of determined
traffic heading south

who disappeared from view
barrelled into nowhere
flung into an unsuspecting moment
while we held our breath
until a burst of feathers
proclaimed her demise.

And when she lay, roadside
as we all swept past -
her rocket-lolly beak, her stillness,
those ungainly lady legs akimbo,
her black flamenco plumage
lifting in the swish
of speeding cars -

I should have pulled in,
scooped up her muddled form
and, cupping the tiny head
heavy on its loose-string neck,
breathed to her
of river, reeds and sky,
her young jibbing back and fore
upon the water.

Jane Lovell

Deborah Vass

Deborah Vass

The Peregrine Falcons of York Minster

Best observed from Dean's Park
(bring binoculars and stand well back
so you don't get a crick in your neck),
Mr and Mrs Minster are high up
on the North West Tower,
on the balcony or on a grotesque.
The falcon prefers *The Thoughtful Man*
who, for centuries, has stroked his chin
and ignored the crowds below,
the tiercel sits on the eroded carving
the other side of the belfry
but then he's the smaller of the two,
less powerful, more easy going
with a neater and cleaner look
even when fluffed up and relaxing.
It's the female who hunts the pigeons
which nest on that ledge in Stonegate
just behind the stone cat above JW Knowles
Stained Glass, Leaded Lights, Decorations.
Look out or your chicks will be
snatched and whisked to a nest
where the fledglings will soon take
their first scary flight from the House of God.

Carole Bromley

Pigeon & Parakeet

Pigeon and Parakeet meet one day in Trafalgar Square.
There's a protest happening and people are wearing green
to show feelings about what they're rallying against or for.
Parakeet is posing for photos as everyone wants to hashtag
#evenbirdswantchange.

Pigeon is feeling a little on the outside to be honest.
This is the place where she's always felt at home,
the grey camouflage of her feathers verifying commuters'
misgivings of having missed out on a great life elsewhere,
like Hawaii or even Devon.

Today is different, Pigeon is no comfort for anyone.
Parakeet has limited sympathy for Pigeon.
She remembers when Pigeon pecked most of a baguette
she'd been saving for her new chicks to enjoy.
Pigeon thought it had been carelessly discarded
but on realising her mistake, never apologised
nor brought replacement nourishment for Parakeet and family.

Pigeon sees someone spray-painting a placard,
she hops over there like worms are being roasted
and despite her dubious spatial awareness,
is soon flying straight into the gush of green.
Pigeon becomes the one everyone wants a picture of,
she shows how anything really is possible
if you take a leap into the unknown.
She flaps her wings for any flash
and her stomach grows crumb heavy.

Parakeet flutters undisturbed now,
wondering how a pigeon sprayed green
could be more exciting than a bird who is actually just green.
But she's used to the strangeness of humans
and she was finding the noise all a little too much anyway.
She flies off into the trees of Pall Mall to spy on the Queen,
see if the window is open just enough to sneak in
pick up for her new nest some of those shiny stones
her grandparents said reminded them of home.

Sabrina Mahfouz

Paul Kielty

The birds

I
I wish I remembered only birds and not blood. They flew into a tree and stopped their song. The neighbour's head shoved into a glass door until it shattered. Copenhagen, 2002. The birds swooped around his body in a circle before disappearing. They were the last image before the sound of an ambulance we didn't see. Mother pulled us off the balcony. The birds left. They too had been changed.

II
How many dead birds have there been this month alone? I stopped counting. I left no time to mourn the pigeon I nearly stepped on and then hurriedly walked past. I wanted to cry for it, to move it, give it a burial and a name.

III
Shopping bags are held close here. Hayes Town, London, 2003. Pigeon central. It's no secret. They're unwanted. They come together or not at all. Where did they come from in these numbers? I watched a man extend his foot. He translated the bird, its movement, its cry, into everything trying to eat the town alive. How did I get here? His extended foot and prayer, protection against pests.

IV
The day a white girl threatened to call the police it was because her father owned the park and she didn't want me in it. An anger, not mine, spread. We were face to face but which one of us screamed and scared away the birds? I watched as they flew over our heads.

V
When I say I'm leaving because I can't live where nobody wants us, mother says *I'll die without you and you'll die without me and we have to be together to survive.*

VI
I woke to a garden full of birds and watched them from the window. Some were perched on the trampoline, others on the washing line, some on grass.

VII
What matters is that they found me, forgave the violence, wanted to forget.

Amaal Said

Katrinka Wilson

  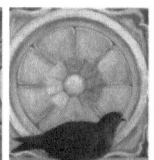  

Feral Pigeons

You'll see them in any town,
scratching a rough and frowned-upon existence
in the gaps, gathered around that eccentric
who loves to break bread and bylaws for them.

Someone has labelled them; 'chequer,
blue bar, pied, white, grizzle,' and so on.
You might see subtle kaleidoscopic
cloudscapes, hazy planet surfaces, rainbows,

but always the asking fool's gold eyes,
always the deep pink feet, some of which
are lacking toes, or have fused into
unsightly scabby blobs to hobble on.

You'll wonder if they've been caught in the netting,
or pierced by the plastic spikes that aim, but fail,
to keep the pigeons out of the best and sheltered
spaces. And then you'll turn your mind away.

Mark Totterdell

  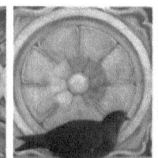  

Adele Pound

Living

I don't miss my feet.
They'd still be intact
if I didn't live in the Smoke.
But why would I live in the country?
I'd be one skinny, bored pigeon.
All those yukky trees.
I get by on these stumps.
I'm either in the air, eating, or asleep.

Paulie lost his on some wire,
like so many, poking trash for kicks;
bit of wire winds round, tangles tight,
blood cuts off and your foot's gone.
But mine went when I caught that thing
going round, standing in everyone's shit
under the railway bridge.
It's where it's at.
I'm not going to miss out.
I know the risks.
I saw it happen to Gloria too.
We all get it sooner or later.
It's my decision, my body.
I deserve some fun.
I'd hate to die of FOMO.

Steph Morris

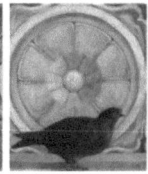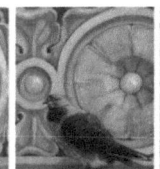

Peter Tinkler

Bird Watching

I spot him near the precinct,
his plumage distinct

by its raggedness,
a grey-coated shabbiness

worn through all weathers,
his feet time-withered

in their splay-toed shuffle.
He grubs on, unruffled

by retail footfall,
past the market stalls,

lucky-dipping in litter bins
for gold and glittered things,

and some lunch,
a grease-smeared treasure hunt

among burger wrappers and coffee cups.
Meanwhile those higher up

in the order of pecking,
stick their necks in,

keep their beaks out,
find another shamefaced route.

I take flight, too. A sudden lurch,
a few flaps, and I'm perched

on a gargoyle, west side of St Hugh's:
my bird's eye view.

I can see everything.
I polish my feathers, clean my wings.

He's outside M&S
in his sleeping bag nest.

Brian Bilston

Adele Pound

Town birds

When pigeons leave the land
abandoning their fields of gold
for richer pickings in the town,

great clouds of grey
threaten to obliterate
the sun; while splatch

and splodge of slimy
excrement traces crazy patterns
over all the pavements underfoot;

feathered flocks increasing exponentially
not by magpie bullying or jay's
tendency to infanticide

but by simpler means
of pilfering the food supply
and unrestrained libido,

while their soft insistent cooing
reminds us they're related to the
not-so-very-gentle, not-so-peaceful dove.

Alwyn Marriage

Unexpected Items

From time to time, a pigeon (let's call her Kate)
swoops in through the sliding doors of Smith's on Market Street.
She picks out a greetings card *(blank, for your own message)*
and takes it in her beak to the self-service till
where she shits generously as the machine bleats
of unexpected items in the bagging area.

Once in a while, another pigeon (Jim)
swoops in just the same and lately,
Liz, Ed and Phil have also taken
to occasionally popping in.

Gibson, the branch manager, thinks it's all the same bird.
Flapping around the shop floor, he doesn't notice
the singular shades of grey, the distinctive flecks of gold
in each iris, the unique shape of every tail.

He'll realise his mistake on the day he catches Kate
and dispatches her to one of the black plastic bins out back.
An hour later he'll be flying around after four birds at once
who'll make off with a biro each and a small pocket diary
while Gibson gives up and calls Head Office.

There'll be an email. Procedures.
A situation to be addressed
or questions will be asked.

As I spray the bagging area
with a diluted anti-bacterial solution,
I run over a few questions of my own.
Who are the cards for?
Why did Kate always choose Monet's lilies
or New Yorker cartoons?
Could *those filthy thieving creatures*
simply wish to send a friendly greeting and,
in the absence of currency, pay us with what they have to give?

Blank, for your own message.
Gets me wondering what occasions pigeons celebrate
that our ample greetings card industry
hasn't thought to create.

Shauna Robertson

Sky Rat

If the bird were a human, somebody
would have had a word
by now. *Listen mate, you can't carry on
like this, every morning, the street is busy, people need
to get by.* The bird

is always bold, with his incandescent
purple chest, sky blue crown, nest
to perfect. The skip
on the side of the Old Town road, the road
leading to the castle, is full

of rotting underlay, his new bed. He flaps
large, striped wings in the face of the woman,
who is eating a breakfast sandwich on the edge
of her office wall, he squawks
eager orders to his invisible workers, that land in the ears

of the lawyer, provoking his phone, *there's more
to this than you mate, you'll have to keep it down,* the bird
shits on the flip-flop of a nondescript tourist, who is looking
already for the castle. He carves industry
on the cream, stone face of the church, a series

of markers, pointing to the black-crypt eaves
of his home. If the bird were a human, somebody
would have moved him and his family on. Three school kids
who are afraid of birds, won't cross the road to school, he looms
large, a warning, an excuse, strutting the road closed.

He loots today's final beak-full
of fibres, looks around at his work,
and I'm sure, before retiring to soothe his soft-mouthed
babies with promises and jokes, he catches
me watching, and winks as he goes.

Amelia Loulli

Adele Pound

Sisters of Mercy

flyover pigeon...
the underpass busker strums
bird on a wire

Tim Gardiner

Heathrow Terminal Five

Heathrow Terminal 5,
Only the Fattened Pigeons
not here to fly.

David Rudd-Mitchell

Nothing

The pigeon stalked around the street,
looking for a tasty treat,
perhaps he could scrounge another chip,
but an empty crisp packet was all he could snip.

So he tried to think of where he could find
the half-a-tuna sandwich that was in his mind,
but everywhere he looked, he found
nothing.

Until he spotted a green bin bag
then flapped on over, heart in the swag,
he ripped it open, pouring out stale bread,
he feasted and feasted until he was fed.

The chef came out to dump more courses,
the pigeon felt his stomach was full of horses,
so, heavily he flew away,
wings galloping, afraid

of nothing.

Nico Loulli

Giancarlo Facchinetti

Red Kite in the City

He can't recall blackened crags
peaks stretched dark
over anchored meadows
or cabbaged trees beneath his feet
not fenced and desiccated shadows

he does not know unbroken lakes
nor rivers unbound
by lock and gate
no memories of wild country
his world is tarred, hemmed in slate

he knows no air but clouded soot
no rain, but sleet –
dripped grime, metal
none but writhing city birds, plump
stained dust, strung on lines of cable

yet high, planing quilted screes
he hovers stiff
in torpid wind, hangs
deep rust over steaming streets
owning this, his changing element – still.

Sue Hardy-Dawson

Red Kite

Look up, I tell my son, there's a red kite,
But it looks like a bird; a small misunderstanding,

we count time, weight shifting, breath to breath;
it hovers, dead still, sharp in profile, sky frozen,

cloud platfomed and underside down,
rooks rush around in swift screaming swoops,

it does not move or follow, held high in the air,
whole body intent on watching, for that moment,

when the prey reveals itself, into the open, possible.
Birds do not use grand gestures, wing warfare,

impatient with the thought of freefalling
to transform life into another language;

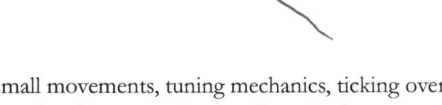

Paul Kielty

small movements, tuning mechanics, ticking over
keeping things running; it will not look away

for anything, this is not a game, the eyes recognise
shifts when they come, and it dives headlong

into the west wind, body saying almost out loud
there it is.

Gusts over greys, past steeple and structural glass,
concrete cliffs, a cityscape,

yet in the eyes, a wilderness,
the great silence, blackness; a starless sky.

Ali Jones

The robin that sings all night

Getting off the late bus, under sodium lights,
we heard no nightingale but a robin in spate,
high in a bush over-sprawling someone's garden wall.
For him it was day, dusk melding into dawn
with no dark hiatus. The clouds shuffled
across the moon, stars out-shone by the city.
Freight trucks sped by on the clear roads,
drivers hunched back listening to their music,
trailing comet-tails of luminosity.
Condemned like them to a night-shift of song,
the dazzled bird proclaimed his territory to the yellow skies.

Derek Sellen

Andrea Robinson

Tony Hay

The waiting room

It was a mistake to come alone.
Though the chairs are soft and the room cool,
she sits stiffly, hot at the neck
waiting her turn.

This is uncertainty, not rest -
the waiting to know
stretches her out
reduces her to the sum of the day so far:
the crude x inked on her skin
the machine squeezing her breast
the kind consultant's steady, hard words
If, then. If ... then ...

She is too tense for magazines
which only look to the future,
to empty, gentle days to fill
with renovations, cruises, next season's colour
she can't bear to turn the pages.

As the clock ticks she sees
through the glass a flicker of wing:
a robin, pecking at the top step of the fire escape
(where she's seen the nurses have their lunch)
her children's favourite, waiting with her,
surely the bird of Christmas, kindness, hope.

Rosemary Appleton

I'm dim

In the winter a robin popped by
each time I got into some digging,
cheeky, and all he wanted was worms,
but good company. I'd be out
to escape people and central heating
and he kept quiet, in a matey way.

Come spring I took in more robins,
and I'm dim about mating
and couply stuff, and maths,
but even I twigged quickly
it was just two, nipping in and out
of the shaggiest patch of ivy.

With the leaves down ivy is the only cover.
I see the fireman's tower, the blocks,
the Wodge, the Dollop, the Insult, the lot,
and the litter the weeds hide all summer.
Also ivy berries are the only thing
the lard-arsed pigeons leave.

Hectic busy fetching stuff, the robins.
Kept seeing them at Wickes. I peeked
at the nest: light wooden weave, infilled
and insulated. He started feeding her up
like a mad thing, Tesco's every day, then the eggs
popped! Now they were feeding little ones,

in and out of the ivy like little *Rosinenbomber*,
the pair of them. This was after a winter
from hell and even in summers from heaven
I forget whether the neighbours' kids
are at nursery or doing A' levels,
but I was gripped. My babies too.

Must have been under another duvet cloud
when it happened. Spring is horrible.
I remember a load of magpie racket
but I just turned the music up,
which brought banging from next door
so I stuck my anti-magpie earplugs in.

And I can't bear to finish this story –
you know where it's heading, right?
I didn't. I dimly registered a change.
No coming and going from the ivy.
The robin couple hopping around
at a loose end, a loss.

My Mum explained, that's what magpies do.
They're nest raiders. It's nature.
Bollocks to nature, I said.
I'd have been the first to go.
It nearly happened, as it goes.
How would you have liked that?

Steph Morris

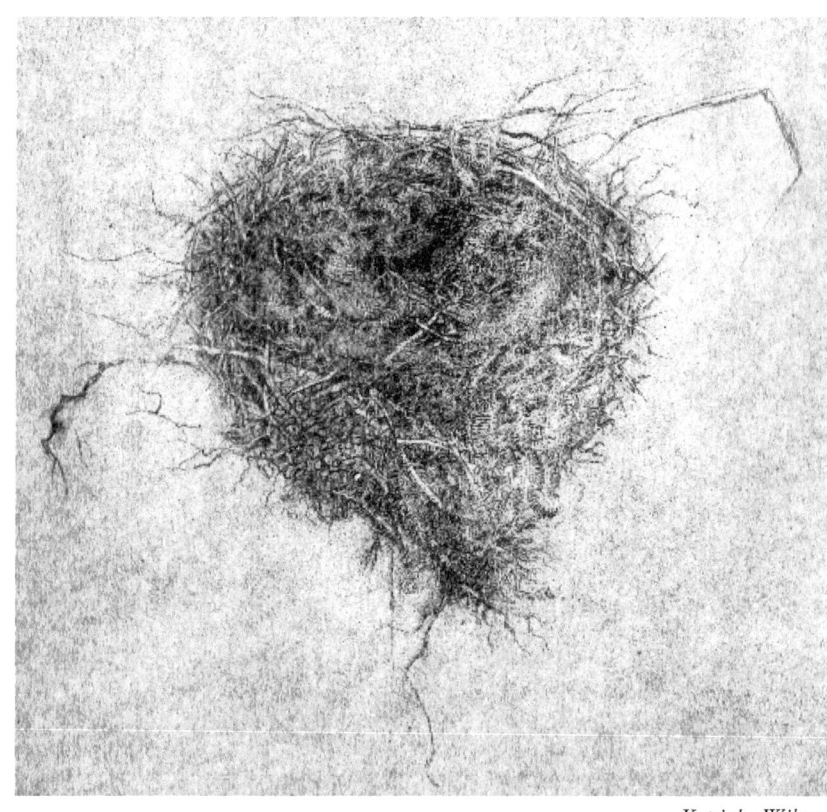

Katrinka Wilson

morning in the tired city

last night's storm now just heavy dew
on the scrubland by our house

and a rook   crossing the road
slowly   limping   like a man

on crutches   looking as though
he has been waiting all night

for a ceasing of the traffic
and on the pavement he has crossed from

a broken black umbrella
which perhaps   the rook thinks   could be

an older brother   wings akimbo
flight interrupted by a car

and hobbling from the muddy grave
of his baggy   windtorn twin

he pauses for a moment
lifts up his head   releases

his throaty voice of rust   cuts dead
the singing that's welcoming the dawn

Andrew McMillan

Eileen Schaer

Inland Gulls

1. **Arrival**

For years it was a few Black-headed gulls snickering in from Llyn Mawr,

        neat   masked   watchers
                                stationed on lamp posts

then Common gulls
        drifted in
            always from the north like memories of snow.

Teatimes they squalled the heat haze
                      turning
                town to a snow-globe

landing raucously in chorus lines at fast food joints

        cruising picnic sites to hustle bins

                and swashbuckle pickings in the river's racing shallows.

Adele Pound

2. **Settling In**

They started staying over
        cwtched up to chimney pots
                ranked themselves on church and cinema roofs.

That summer my student stopped mid-sentence –

Listen! You'd think we were at the seaside, not the centre of town, wouldn't you?

Flocks cracked into classic keening
                as if mourning their landlocked state
and we Desert Islanded the rest of the lesson
              Maths and Art and History washed around us.

August, they settled at the shopping mall
              copulating by the spinning fins of air-con
keeping us all awake with cries more frivolous than sirens
              more insistent than boy racers' intermittent squeals

and sudden revved up backfirings.

3. **Soap Opera**

Omo   Persil   Daz

I think town gulls are the dreams incarnate of early admen
the ones who boasted they'd add *brightness to whiteness*
battling detergents' white supremacy.

I watch the birds on sports fields, tramping
for worms and staying unspattered, so unlike
my school socks which wicked dirt and washed grey.

They squabble takeaway trays streaked
with gory sauce, wade through gravel
and garbage and they always come up

    glittering like the *Tide*   dazzling as *Surf*.

4. **Polymorphs**

There are elements of Everybird in gulls
the soar and stoop of falcons, songbirds'

jab-propulsion, pigeon strut and stage
swagger, waders' slow, reflective preening

echoes of us too   the cries of all our broken
brawling nights   flight patterns scattering
like stray thoughts and suddenly switching to fluent formation.

Timeless gulls:
                traces of pterodactyl
                                    and targeted war drone.

Chris Kinsey

Rob Turner

Andrea Robinson

A Shared Call

We wake at night. Gull call
cacophony, hailing
dawn.

From my window
the whitening caws, the grey raising
of puffy wings
                        stretching
across   grey rooftops,
as young birds bicker
to be fed.
In the next room, my son
woken by the birds
echoes out his own
emergent cries,
                        ready
to be fed.

I and the gulls rise
together, answering

life.

Nick Falkowski

Gulls

No one objects to gulls that follow trawlers,
that wheel against a purple and tempestuous sky
that scream for the delights of dying fish
as the swollen net is hauled aboard.

No one detests the gulls that mob behind the plough,
white and scrabbling in the dark, turned soil.
No one grudges them their feast:
the glistening worms,
the crunch of frantic beetles,
the pulpy explosions of leather -jackets.

But should they venture into our preserve,
lured by discarded burgers, chips or worse,
should they presume to raise their young
on our accommodating roofs,
and greet each sunrise with parental row,
then will we cry for slaughter.

We will not love these gastronomic migrants
unless they cease to interfere
with our alfresco guzzling of ice cream,
our need to sleep, replete, well past the dawn.

Gordon Gibson

Therese Lee

Adele Pound

Ruffled feathers

Slumpshouldered, I stagger
home in summer bright. I wish
I'd caught the last bus, wish I could
afford a taxi. Ahead I catch the edge
of a ruckus. Angry cries, coarse curses,
harsh insults crowd the air. A fight
blocks the path. The gang squabble lunge,
ricochet. Sharp jabs, hard blows.
Heads cocked, feet at the ready, they
prancepounce. Eyes narrow focus
Broad backed, sturdy legs braced, they
bouncegrab burgers,tussle buns, batter
fish. Outright champion, a burly
chap, *Larus argentatus,* struts off.
Grey chicken skin flaps from yellow beak.
I wish I'd the money for chips.

Finola Scott

Adele Pound

'Seagull's swooping attack in Maryport delays mail delivery'

Every day you patrolled our street,
        defending your adolescent chicks,
who squatted, plump, on two parked cars,
        awaiting their next food parcel.

One day I forgot your presence
        and foolishly strolled past your chimney roost.
Your face a furious paper cut-out,
        you plummeted earthwards.

I swore and flinched
        as your armoured claws skimmed my scalp,
your wingfeather quills
        speared the air.

A millisecond before skull contact,
        you fired a Jackson Pollock splat right down my back –
a gooey archipelago
        of khaki, brown and white.

I heard your harpy shriek,
        sensed your yellow eye lasering my skull,
felt a membrane tear
        between my world and yours.

Kelly Davis

The Seagulls Have Been Canceled

after Maya Catherine Popa's 'The Bees Have Been Canceled'

On the train platform, a toddler
does not stumble toward a seagull,
both pudgy hands reaching to touch
the whitest body, that slightly hooked beak.

In the city centre hotels, sleepers wake
at the chirp of their alarms rather than
the gulls' spiraling, sunrise cries.

As I walk to work, my pace quickens,
my body curls inward: such is the great
weight of these emptied skies.

Carrie Etter

Caller

A soft thump on the glass
made me look up from my desk.

On the roof
a sparrow, concussed in the furrow
of terracotta tiles.

He'd hit the window
hard, sat blinking in a downy drift
as if the world was new.

I worried for his jigged spine
the knuckle of his skull
and thought of you

in your helmet and leathers.
He tilted his eye
to mine, puffed his chest and flew.

Roy Marshall

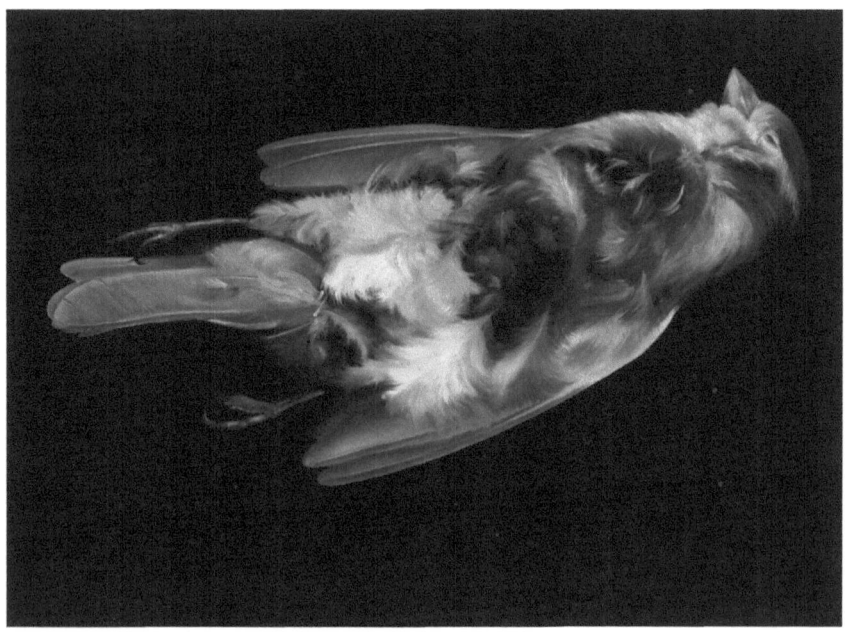

Mark Sheeky

Andrew Tyzack

A reason for faking it

I'm walking past the long hedge,
when you suddenly pop out and wait
five human paces down the lane,
hop a little, flutter in the air then stop,
half-turn so that one eye is looking back
at me. *Come on, come on* you chirrup cheekily.

You fly a little further on, then drop your wing
onto the ground as though it might be sprained.
I'm gaining on you now, so off you fly again,
glance back, then satisfied, rise up above the hedge,
returning to the point at which we met, where
loud and hungry mouths are waiting for a mother's care.

Alwyn Marriage

One Called Paul

Five drab juveniles land outside my window;
goth eyeliner, raucous and rucking over territory,
fouling up my window ledge, five floors high.

In the shadows of murmuration, three leave suddenly,
startle the two, who look to each other and draw closer,
before the larger wings it to thousands in late city skies.

The smallest catches reflections in the high rise glass,
checks its rag tag feathers for signs of iridescence
emerging in the half-light of a noisy urban dusk.

But through my window, I see only reluctance in movement.
I wonder if this one's worried; ill-prepared to join in
and just needs a little more time to practise.

Jonathan Humble

Deborah Vass

Penny Hodson

Starlings

They come in constellations of oily stars
Hell's spangled minions, shrieking rebels

with a cause. Clamouring locusts on lawns
mugging bread, bullying sparrows. Thrush

giving sly glances. Anvil beaked, skulking
back to the hedge, in their biker jackets

squabble with thorns, torn grey, dewy webs.
But sky's their thing, there they bloom in

kaleidoscope columns, dark nimbus, the
cackled black flames of gathering dusk

bleed and reform, in buttery light, to settle
their backward autumn on trees of soot.

Sue Hardy-Dawson

Dan Davis

Murmuration

As I joined the five pm soldiers
Marching slowly homewards,
My thousand yard stare is distracted
By The flit of shadows across the pavement
Then the sound of a pulsing fluttering beat.
I look up to see starlings soaring across the dusky sky.

Like me these birds are bound for home
Unlike me they are dancing.
A thousand pairs of wings move in dazzling unison
Formation perfect they whirl and swirl,
Each part of the whole instinctively
Knowing their place in this stunning display.

As I watch sable shooting stars plummet towards the earth
Then at the last second soar skyward again
Seemingly blissfully ignorant of gravity's grasp.
Dark waves slam against each other,
Splintering into a thousand living shards
Quickly reforming into a turbulent whole.

On the bus home my thoughts twist and turn
As I replay avian acrobatics,
While my fingers dance on my phone.
Providing the answer I seek.
"Murmaration," I mumble to myself,
The word doesn't do justice to what I just witnessed.

Richard Archer

Murmuration

A cloud of iron filings
pulled across a November sky
by an invisible magnetic force,
hidden on the horizon,
before the light begins to fade.

A thousand paper fans rustling
above the rooftops of a northern town.
Commuters rushing down station steps
stop in their tracks and stare
at this synchronised display.

A starling swarm swoops en masse,
bulging and shrinking,
rising like smoke from a genie's lamp,
wrapping like a giant ribbon around itself.
A perfect choreography of flight.

This murmuring congregation
seems ignorant of the audience below.
They make their own applause
with beating wings and eerie cries,
shimmering as they mesmerise.

Linda Kurowski

Linda Kurowski

Swallows on Oxford Street

I took the shirt back
but they told me I was a day too late for a refund,
then, when they saw it had a stain,
refused to even do an exchange.

Deflated, I left the store
with the shirt still in my hand
but, just as I did,
a shock of swallows,
shooting out of a side street,
made me raise my eyes
for the first time ever
above the ground-level grind
of black cabs and big crowds
and bulk commerce.

To think, I'd never looked up before –
my eyes having previously
always been kept in line
by endless shop displays –
but, amazingly, on this first occasion
that my gaze had been diverted upwards,
I was getting to see,
just three floors up,
a flock of swallows,
flying in perfect formation,
swooping and swirling above my head,
then settling into position
on the grey-stone ledges
and pediments of windows
on the top two storeys
of the red-brick building
housing H&M and Uniqlo.

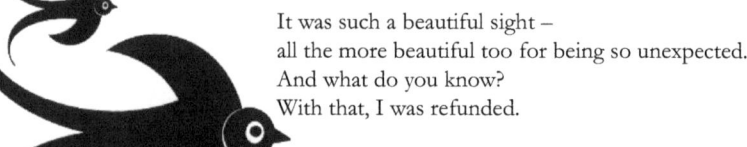

It was such a beautiful sight –
all the more beautiful too for being so unexpected.
And what do you know?
With that, I was refunded.

Thomas McColl

Paul Kielty

Paul Kielty

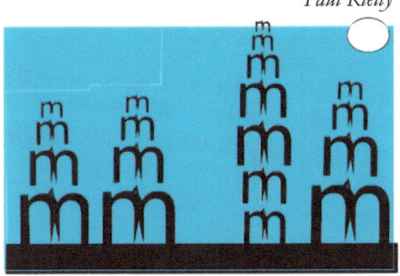

A Festival of Swallows - Hyde Park

Summer city festival,
and as the crowd gathers on a warm June evening
a flypast of swallows perform overhead,
a breathtaking spectacle of
aerial acrobatics, swooping, darting, snapping
wind-borne flies, tail streamers forked,
pointed wings arrowing through air,
a steel-blue flash.

But as the atmosphere reverberates
with bass rhythms and drumbeats,
they withdraw to the quiet of the Serpentine,
skimming the water, dipping low over the lake.

And as the dusk dims into dark indistinctness
their twittering cries quiet
as they roost in reed beds.

By September's Proms in the Park
the swallows are gone, drawn
to the warmth of the south,
Provencal, the Pyrennees, Palma, Marrakesh, the Sahara desert,
Lake Chad, Masai Mara, Limpopo, Transvaal.

And as Christmas lights shimmer
 through dense London smog
and early morning grass is spiked with frost,
they scythe through African air,
heat reflecting off burning sand,
snatching a black speck
from the back of an elephant,
roosting in maize
when the sun falls fast.

Sue Mackrell

Gordon Yapp

Journey

Oh the draggled darlings, sky urchins
with chestnut summer throats -
who could deny you your urge
for warmth and swarms of easy food?

Drenched with September rain
you clench, unclench the phone wires,
jostle and flit away to gorge on insects
from the last warm bricks then back again.

Under your feathers there is a pulse you know
you must follow over dream-charted deserts.
Without trust you will fall to earth but still
comes the unanswerable call to be elsewhere.

Now the empty phone wires sagging with rain
recall your restless, negligible weights.

Jeff Phelps

Swan Over Swalwell Roundabout

The numb drudge of our early drag to work is roused
by the suddenness of a huge swan. Every car stops dead.

Low as the bollards, it has come from the Derwent
like some kind of portent, some half-remembered thing

waiting for height to build beneath its span – lift it
beyond this oddball, misfit morning we have found

ourselves together in. Everyone gawping jaw-drop
at this battleship, cumbersome so close to the ground,

wing muscles working billy-o to carry it out of our lives.
Its milky neck outstretches with single-minded aim.

It is going somewhere – not into customer service, retail
madness, office, pen push, *yes sir, no sir, three bags full sir.*

It has got more brains than that. This momentary pause
in traffic is mystical. The golden beak tip parts

the fumey fug as if it were a floated soul, scudding away
from hell. *Take me with you*, I whisper and watch until

the bird is a speck and some impatient body drives
almost into my boot and beeps. It takes a moment

for the four ways to move on. This was a flight path
before it was road – once it would have been flowers.

Jane Burn

Paul Kielty

Sue Spawn

About them

This poem should be about love. It's not.
It concerns the visits of swifts and swallows,

how the former scythes, the latter streams
towards us and both deftly draw warmth, food,
drink from river and hedge.

It is about aerial tricks they play, the displays
of chase, swoop, glide and that courtship and
nesting suggest they may settle.

They require nothing from us, our yearning
is alien. We admire and coax, our hearts rise
with their arrival, they announce

the seasons we desire. This is nothing to them.
They stay beyond reach. We never learn.
In September they dwindle

by October it's finished. Idyll over, the skies
fall silent a moment while they turn, lift off
and leave us to winter alone.

This poem should be about love. It's not.
It's about them.

Lyn White

Sky high

Swifts streaming across the sky screaming
    form, briefly, half a constellation then disperse.

        No time to stop, stay, play; no sooner here
            than off again, almost colliding, then away;

            silhouettes of urgent arrows
                aiming at moving targets no one else can see,

                their taut wings cutting air to slice
            the sky across its widest arc:

        over-excited summer visitors.
        so drunk on speed that legless,

    screeching with hilarity or terror
    while sweeping insects cleanly off the blue.

  I suspect that I, too, would scream,
if I found myself flying that fast.

Alwyn Marriage

Sue Spawn

The Thrush

The morning thrush who just would not stop singing....
filip filip filip codidio codidio quitquiquit tittit tittit tereret tereret tereret

Quite early on a spring morning I could hear
a song thrush singing sprightly, but could not see it.

By an open window I listened to the dawn chorus
like a whole orchestra of different voices

but the thrush was nearer - singing a fine tune
and then repeating it several times over

Then it started its special performance piece
followed by a pause, as if to say, aren't I clever

and just in case you missed it, here it is again
filip filip filip codidio codidio quitquiquit tittit tittit tereret tereret tereret

The thrush has the habit of repeating song phrases
and can even mimic the phone, ring, ring, busy line.

It sang and sang and sang claiming its territory
so I could not take my shower for 20 minutes

Eventually I took my ablutions - believe
it or not the thrush just carried on singing.

Gordon Yapp

Frances Rarehare

A murder of thrushes

The massacre starts when I'm asleep,
and is over long before my feet
in outdoor shoes find evidence -
the soft grey crunch along the path;
the hemispheres that once held life,
now fragile tombstones, uninscribed,
and disappearing with each step.

The songthrushes have fed their notes
once more with snails, battered, dropped -
the paving slabs in place of spoons
for cracking shells; sad wrappers of
this live fast food - or, rather, slow;
escape is not an option here.

So while I dream of futures full
of sun and opportunity,
winged terrorists do what they must -
a mindful slaughter; not with hopes
of paradise to come; no heaven,
just sustenance; the need for food.
And when they've killed, they wake me with
a song that says "I live!"

Brenda Read-Brown

Paul Kielty

Wagtail Swagger

He rolls up
checking out the wildlife
shaking a tail feather at the local cats
bobbing to the beat

His African cousin would come
right into our house
King confidence
He'd take the milk teeth
thrown on the roof by our neighbour's kids
and deliver them fresh gnashers
mincing round like he owned the place

More circumspect (those cats)
The Coventry wagtail
two tone, wily,
combs carparks
quick with a pied flick
searching for the right tick to take
ducking and diving
bobbing and weaving
In the Midlands way.

Andrea Mbarushimana

Adele Pound

Adele Pound

Wolverhampton Wagtails

Salt-and-pepper-slick and picking at crumbs,
they admire themselves in puddles of honey,
strut among wheels, tails working like levers.
Up here, they are church-bell-high,
chests bright as pennies in the peachy dusk.
They circle me in shoals - expand, contract,
like lungs full of pure, pink breath,
a heartbeat of delicate wings.
Grey as exhaust-smoke, as mist that rises
from the canal on December mornings,
they disappear as easily.
As I steer through the concrete sea,
they scatter from the car like fireworks,
like a handful of change.

Cherry Doyle

Lisa Osborne

Woodpecker

Persistence resonating purpose, passion
reminding us of beings without form –

the unmistakable signature, drum
roll tattoo of bill, beating against bark in rhythm.

Yet nowhere is the wryneck to be seen,
camouflaged in the trees. I am not the only one

walking in Highgate Wood with my face upturned,
eyes scanning branches of trees, April bare,

giddy with birds' nests swaying in the wind
perched precariously high up in the air,

caught in crotches of sturdiest oak and hornbeam.
The furious pecking of the Great Spotted fades

as we spot robins, jays, wagtails, starlings,
with many a thought that did not come flying.

The sky-calling, whistling, singing,
the wind-tickled chimes of a charm of finches –
bird chorus celebrates all that is hidden.

Bluebells sleep buried in earthworks,
dreaming of things tired eyes cannot see.

In the distance a fleeting vision of zygodactyl feet,
a mottled woodpecker's profile disappearing.

Shanta Acharya

Drunken Woodpigeons
Mooring. Lyons Boatyard. Birmingham

Woodpigeons came often:
On misted mornings,
in twilights blue shadows.
To coo and rustle through Poplars on the bank.
Grey wings flickered as they clustered,
through leaf-flashes of gold and green.
Burrowed under branch and leaf,
Clung with scaly claws in groups,
clumped like Brussels' sprouts on stems.
Beaks winnowed through ivy,
where berries hung star-shaped clusters,
black, heavy and ripe.
'Pigeons gorged, clung precariously
upside down, wings slumped wide
in lazy intoxication
as they stuffed themselves fat and silly,
dropped greed-loosened orbs
that splattered blue spots onto the ground,
left a mild fungal scent.
Often birds would fall with a thump,
a startled squawk,
a disgruntled flurry of feathers.
To rise, weave along towpath-side,
heads bobbing,
tails wobbling a dip and shimmy,
wings spread for balance.
Made it clear that humans hold no monopoly
on the foibles of too much drink.

Miki Byrne

Paul Kielty

Deborah Vass

Wren Song

Girl on swing
escapes into playground
ear air rush
into sky fiction future
and wren song
wriggling
Small brown feather puff
lyrical explosion
She sings back to it
stuttering clumsy
and they serenade each other
into evening
for years it continues
Tenuously nesting
Girl grows up
swing rusts down
but every wren song since
soars skywards.

Andrea Mbarushimana

Frances Rarehare

Spring in Kew Garden

Pure rapture this panorama of pink,
verging on crimson-maroon to blushing white.

Under the spell of cherry blossoms,
loneliness scatters like particles of dust in light.

A deep silence revives the listening soul
like birdsong beginning inside the egg.

Suddenly lifted on the wings of a warbler's song,
a cuckoo's ecstatic call carries me home.

I am speaking to my mother recovering
from her fall, calibrating her voice against the koels'
singing among the trees in our courtyard.

Or is it the other way round –
birdsong rising in decibels as noise in cities
grow deafeningly loud?

Planes flying over the Royal Botanic Gardens
distract from the peace of ancient trees.

The all-seeing peacocks, their fanned tails quivering
with wild, forlorn calls awaken in me immortal longings –

making it possible to be in two places at once.
I am in Mathura, inside the temple of Krishna,

waiting for a darshan. Outside, proud defenders
of faith and grace, peacocks teach us to be incorruptible,
discover our inner beauty, display our true colours.

I came into this world with only my shadow,
wake to this magnificent world of love.

Shanta Acharya

Mark Mennell

City Bird's Courtship Songs

City birds' mating songs
are shorter,
louder,
and have longer pauses.

To rise above
The drone,
That traffic causes.

It's apt my
City friends
 can all
  relate

This city is no place
To woo a mate.

David Rudd-Mitchell

Distant Cousins

Breaking in my brand new brogues
long wings with hand-stitched welts
I sip and swipe and tap. What else? Then stop
and stare. And stare, pat myself on the back.
And then…
'Don't know its name.
Average size I guess. 'Bit brown, dark grey, 'bit non-descript. 'Bit black?
Lying there. Head flopped to one side
eye popped out and fixed.
Beak ajar, peppered with flies, mapping its face
as it drifts in
and out of life.

I'm a distant cousin, twice removed
in soft play, coddled in a high-vis top.
When my phone dies I plug it in
and it wakes up.

Aysar Ghassan

Dan Davis

birds laugh

i walk the subways all the time
in the mornings there are more birds
than cars out
and in the nights the lights fixed on the walls are like
square
amber
disco balls
for the gnats who've come
to party
i like the graffiti sprayed on the walls
of the concrete maze under the city
one wall says i feel fantastic
i passed it on the way back from the hospital one morning
the birds laughed
and so did i.

Rhian Elizabeth

Close encounters of the bird kind

At the start of my journey on a suburban road
a pigeon stood in my way refusing to move,
then his Kamikaze mate flew towards my car;
I stalled, then ducked which was no use at all.
I breathed a sigh of relief as they soared away

A one-for-sorrow magpie sitting on a wall, made me look
all around, in the sky and on the ground. I needed joy,
but he was alone, so I had to chant "Good morning my lord,
good morning my Lord," or the sword of Damocles
might have fallen on my head. All was fine.

I continued until a swan followed by her cygnets,
waddled into the road; I braked, no harm was done
and I drove on until I reached home, relieved;
the birds and I were still intact, all except for the inwards
of one, spattered on my roof; wishing me good luck?

Janet Jenkins

Ann Bridges

Frances Rarehare

Birdsong

Once we knew spring
she came like us shy
slowly quickened
into misty summer

buds yellow stars
opened green eyes
rain softened days
rose earlier warmer

now dawn is always
square suns in lines
rise humming we
fledge bitter half song

in boxed galaxies
flickering lights

once we knew night
darkness came often
long silences
owl's hooked cry

before choked wind
trees lying broken
before they caged us
lit the sleeping sky.

Sue Hardy-Dawson

Dawn Chorus in July

Restive, on top of the sheet
the window open

it's the singing that keeps you awake
these airless nights

more cobbled together than it was
but still stitched tight to the point of puckering, enveloping,

heavy on your skin.
Hold it to the light and the dawn pokes fingers

through its knotted, slubby weave,
the pulls and snags

colouring wisps of faded song
the brown of wrens, blue tits' cerulean

a blackbird's
ruinous dark farewell.

Deborah Harvey

Frances Rarehare

Before the Birds Took Off

They were everywhere, always under our feet.
You could barely skip a step without trampling a toucan
or kicking a cuckoo.

And boy, were they moody.
Sweet tweets and cheerful chirps?
Forget it! Our feathered friends were *hacked off*
at the lack of space and getting more feathered,
less friendly, by the second.

Bluejays bickered bitterly
over cormorants causing traffic jams
while magpies refused
to use the designated lanes,
grousing they were beak-to-tail
with nine hundred nightingales.
Wrens wrestled for legroom
on the rammed-to-the-rafters railways
and coots cowered, dodging the ducks
pecking at their backs about the transport cuts.
Public parks were knee-deep in swans
while every parrot, peewee, pelican, pigeon
pounded the towns' pavements, day and night.

Something had to give, and it did.
Still, sometimes I wonder what life would be like
were it us, and not them, who took flight.

Shauna Robertson

by the time it gets dark

I thought there were few birds in my city
perhaps a vestige of Sixties Yelverton Road:
Daring breakfast pigeons dodging cars
for white breadcrumbs. Scattered above,
the morning swoop and swirl of Starlings
a shadow of dark silk unfurled;
a dancing community, on the breeze.

They are here.

Not like some Hitchcock haunting
of a school playground climbing frame,
but living between traffic and trains. On
leafy spaces; the welcome branches trilling
with their tunes. Thames River side, under
crevices, in old guttering, on terrace chimneys.
Cooing in concrete. Between colonnades,

they are here.

The undersong of the cities walkways.
A persistent chatter behind the clatter
of human sounds. Hooting n hollering five
Burgess Park Canada Geese fly low
by the trees, under planes on the Gatwick flight
path. Cycling across bushes - a surprise
susurrus of sparrows in rush hour flit and flutter.

They are here

Sarah Yates

Sarah Yates

at lunchtime. I'm eating bammy, broccoli and
fish. I look up into mirror black-eyed-beads.
Outside my open kitchen window,
an alighting feathery visitation: two pigeons
sporting on Swanmead's white bark branches,
of shimmering leaves, producing mellow
phrases from their small bodies. Flying -

there they are!

Out from among the cover of trees, Old
Kent Road's cheeky magpies. Two turquoise
tails twitching, they spy the glittering green
fabric of the Mosque flying - Allah Akbar!
On the Peabody estate's open green Starlings
singing from slate. Pigeons peep from parapets,
with deep midnight purple iridescent necks.

They are here.

Throbbing under Bricklayers Arms flyover.
Sprightly sparrows round Tower Bridge Road bins.
Listening, I'm now serenaded by their tunes
around town. My biggest surprise?
The housing co-op's hovering Garden Warbler
(put me in mind of a slow Hummingbird!)
by the shivering whispers of silver birch leaves.

They are here,

colonising leafy city square's with song.
A sauntering crown of crows, caw and 'cauk'
across their feeding field of Burgess Park.
While summer holiday boys in football shirts,
are run ragged up, down, and around the incline.
Lake side a maturing team of mallards molt

fawn-brown baby-down, for striking emerald green.

They are here,

more than I'd imagined. Not just stately wood pigeons
charcoal grey, khaki brown. But the citron yellow
flash of a Tit's tiny throat; Curious shiny black magpies;
A Seagull swooping onto a chimney. All off the Old Kent
Road. With these sights and sounds, my view of my city
 - forever transformed. By the time it gets dark again,
I know the morning will sing.

Dorothea Smartt

Sarah Yates

Birds!

At dusk the bird-swarm hits the sky, for one
last crazy flight; hot-blooded skaters,
they carve their figures-of-eight again at dawn
after the silencing night's hiatus.

The park, the street, the yard, they're there,
issuing their calls of ownership and mating,
warbling a chanson to the air
or hidden in the bushes altercating.

Defying wire meant to keep them off a ledge
or ersatz falcons flapping from a mast,
they spatter lime on tower, dome, bridge,
a warmer place to have your roost

than forest, scrub or marsh. They spy out
launch-pads and flightpaths in urban haze;
in their season, calibrated displays
by starling squadrons make even blasé city kids

cry out: Birds! Birds! Birds!

Derek Sellen

Biographies

Shanta Acharya was born and educated in India, awarded a doctoral degree in English from Oxford and served as a Visiting Scholar at Harvard. The author of eleven books, her latest is *Imagine: New and Selected Poems* (HarperCollins, India; 2017). Founder of Poetry in the House, Shanta hosted a series of monthly poetry readings at Lauderdale House in London from 1996 to 2015. www.shantaacharya.com

George Aird is a writer and editor based in the North West. His poems have been published in magazines including The North Magazine, Ink, Sweat and Tears, Eye Flash Poetry (Issues 1 & 2), Goodbye Zine, Cake Magazine, and Maybe Later Press. In Autumn 2017 he co-edited issue ten of Butcher's Dog Magazine, and is currently working on a debut pamphlet of poems.

Rosemary Appleton has had her poems published in Mslexia, The Fenland Reed, Spontaneity and *#refugeeswelcome* (an Eyewear Press anthology). She writes in snatched, coffee-fuelled moments in the wilds of East Anglia.

Richard Archer is a poet from Walsall who writes on many subjects tending to focus on anything that crosses his path and catches his eye. He has been writing poetry since he left school many years ago and is chairman of the Walsall Poetry Society.

ATM (ATMstreetart) paints endangered species street art, using urban walls as a stark reminder of the species that once lived here, and could again with regeneration of habitats. By bringing colour and beauty to neglected areas the hope is to inspire active participation in further environmental improvements, and to help inspire a transformation of our towns, cities and countryside by renaturing and rewilding.

Brian Bilston is a poet clouded in the pipe smoke of mystery, who shares his poems on Twitter and other social media platforms. His first collection of poetry, *You Took the Last Bus Home* was published in 2016.
https://brianbilston.com/

Ann Bridges studied Illustration at The North Wales College of Art and Design (Glyndwr University), specialising in drawing and printmaking. Having lived and worked in Wales for twenty five years Ann is currently based near Sevenoaks in Kent.
www.ann-bridges.com

Carole Bromley lives in York. She has three collections with Smith/Doorstop : *A Guided Tour of The Ice House*, *The Stonegate Devil* and *Blast Off!* (for children 7-10)
www.carolebromleypoetry.co.uk

Jane Burn is a poet and artist who adores nature and often centres her work upon it. Her poems have been published in many magazine and anthologies. She lives with her family and animals in a self-sufficient, off-grid settlement in Northumberland for nine months of the year.

Miki Byrne has written 3 poetry collections, and had work included in over 170 poetry magazines and anthologies. She has read on TV and on Radio many times. Miki is active on the spoken word scene in Cheltenham and ran a poetry writing group at The Roses Theatre, Tewkesbury. She began performing her poems in a bikers club in Birmingham. Miki is disabled and lives near Tewkesbury, Gloucestershire.

Ken Cockburn is a poet and translator based in Edinburgh, where he runs poetry walks in the city's Old Town. A new collection, *Floating the Woods*, appears in 2018. http://kencockburn.co.uk

Tina Cole is a retired education consultant who lives on the Herefordshire/ Worcestershire border. Her poems have been published in Mslexia, Aesthetica, & Decanto; The Guardian & several anthologies. Her first collection, *I Almost Knew You*, was published in 2015. She is the organiser of Tenbury Young Peoples Poetry Competition – poetryintenbury.org.

Dan Davis was born in 1962, and has lived and worked in London all of his life, he trained as an illustrator at St Martins School of Art (the old building in Long Acre) and a completed a short post graduate at the Royal College of Art. He worked as an illustrator working for magazines, book publishers and record companies, before deciding to be a fine artist. Dan has always been a keen birdwatcher.

Black Redstart, Dan Davis

Kelly Davis lives in Maryport, on the West Cumbrian coast, and works as a freelance editor. Her poems have been commended in the 2016 Fire River Poets and the Cannon Poets Sonnet or Not competitions, published in Mslexia, Poetry Scotland, and anthologized in *Poetry for Performance* (The Playing Space) and *Write to Be Counted* (The Book Mill). She chairs sessions at the annual Words by the Water Festival in Keswick, Cumbria.

Cherry Doyle lives near Cannock Chase. Her work has appeared in Southlight, The Cadaverine, Ink, Sweat & Tears, and others. She helps to run Blakenhall Writers in Wolverhampton, and is completing a degree in Creative Writing.

Rhian Elizabeth was born in 1988 in the Rhondda Valley, South Wales, and now lives in Cardiff. Her novel, *Six Pounds Eight Ounces* (Seren, 2014), was shortlisted for The International Rubery Book Award. Her debut poetry collection will be published by Parthian in Spring 2018.

Carrie Etter has three published poetry collections: *The Tethers* (Seren, 2009), won the London New Poetry Prize, *Divining for Starters* (Shearsman, 2011), and *Imagined Sons* (Seren, 2014), shortlisted for the Ted Hughes Award for New Work in Poetry by The Poetry Society. She also edited anthologies; & has a pamphlet of short stories, *Hometown* (V. Press, 2016). She is Reader in Creative Writing at Bath Spa University and lives in Bath.

Giancarlo Facchinetti is a musician & multi instrumentalist, home recordist, visual & sound artist; and recently podcast editor/ producer for Fair Acre Press. He has orchestrated & performed with an astrophysicist and two poets in a mobile planetarium dome in *The History of the Universe in 45 Minutes*. His artwork is shown in *Painting by Pixels* in Shropshire, 2018.

Nick Falkowski is a British Poet, originally from the Isle of Wight, now living in Birmingham, UK. He has degrees in Philosophy and Classics, and has been published in several poetry magazines. His passions include writing, travelling, and exploring the city around him.

Heather Fowler has a daughter and son and four grandchildren. She worked as an English and Drama teacher and discovered painting upon retirement. Working on art has opened her eyes to a whole new world.

Tim Gardiner is an award-winning ecologist, poet and children's author from Manningtree, Essex. His haiku have been published in literary magazines including Frogpond, Modern Haiku and The Heron's Nest. His first collection of poetry, *Wilderness*, was published by Brambleby Books in 2015, with a second, *On the Edge*, in 2017.

Aysar Ghassan lives in the West Midlands. His work has featured in magazines such as Abridged, Critical Survey and Zarf as well as in *Writing Lives Together* - an anthology published by University of Leicester's Centre for New Writing. In 2016 Aysar undertook a camouflage-themed poetry residence at Leamington Spa Art Gallery & Museum.

Gordon Gibson lives in south-west Scotland. After 20 years as a lecturer in higher education, he now writes full-time. His work, poetry and prose fiction, has appeared in a number of print and online publications. He has been an enthusiastic birdwatcher for the past 40 years.

Sue Hardy-Dawson is a widely published dyslexic poet/illustrator. She has a First Class BA Honours and her first solo collection, *Where Zebras Go* (Otter-Barry Books) was long listed for the 2017 North Somerset Teachers' Book Award. A second book *Apes to Zebras* (Bloomsbury, with Roger Stevens and Liz Brownlee) is due out in 2018.

Deborah Harvey's poetry collections, *Communion* (2011), *Map Reading for Beginners* (2014), and *Breadcrumbs* (2016), are published by Indigo Dreams, while her historical novel, *Dart*, appeared under their Tamar Books imprint in 2013. She finds inspiration for her writing in the landscapes and stories of her native West Country.

Jen Hawkins is an Aromatherapist and teacher. She lives in Shropshire, where the natural outstanding beauty inspires her and influences her writing. Jen's first book *Synergy of the Seasons*, a simple go-to-guide for seasonal health and wellbeing, was published in 2017.

Tony Hay lives in Birmingham, having studied animation at the University of Wolverhampton. A keen photographer - particularly of light and disused urban architecture; he will be part of a group art exhibition in Shropshire in 2018.

Bird, Tony Hay

Penny Hodson has been drawing and painting since childhood and gained a BA (Hons) in Fine Art in 1995. Penny mainly produces portraits and is also interested in landscapes, seascapes and wildlife. She currently lives in Edinburgh.
www.facebook.com/pennyhodsonartist

Jonathan Humble is a teacher in Cumbria. His poetry has appeared in a number of publications, including Ink Sweat & Tears, Obsessed With Pipework, Curlew Calling Anthology, Zoomorphic, *Milestones* Anthology and on BBC Radio. His short stories and poems for children have been published in The Caterpillar and Stew Magazine.

Janet Jenkins is a retired Nursery Head teacher from Staffordshire. She is the leader of The Lichfield Poets and takes part in the group's performances at festivals etc. She also reads at open mic events in her local area. Her poems have been included in literary magazines and anthologies.

Ali Jones is a teacher and mother of three. Her work has appeared in Fire, Poetry Rivals, Strange Poetry, Ink Sweat and Tears, Snakeskin Poetry, Atrium, Mother's Milk Books, Green Parent magazine and The Guardian. Her pamphlets *Heartwood* and *Omega* are forthcoming with Indigo Dreams Press in 2018.

Paul Kielty is an artist, cartoonist, art workshop leader, stand-up comedian and musician. He will be part of a group exhibition at Qube gallery, Oswestry in 2018 and his first book of cartoons will be published in 2018 titled *The Return of the Naive*.

Nadia Kingsley has written poetry pamphlets with David Calcutt: *Road Kill* and *Through the Woods* (the latter also with artist Peter Tinkler); *Lawn Lore*; and *A Year in Herbs* (with herbalist Jayne Palmer). She is editor, and publisher at Fair Acre Press. She co-wrote and performed in e-x-p-a-n-d-i-n-g: the history of the Universe in 45 minutes.

Chris Kinsey's poems have won many prizes – most recently The Thomas Gray Tercentenary Prize, also BBC Wildlife Poet of the Year. She is author of four poetry collections – *Muddy Fox* by The Rack Press was launched in January, 2017. A fifth collection has been commissioned by Fair Acre Press for 2018.

Linda Kurowski writes poems on many subjects and enjoys reading her work at her local spoken word group. Her poetry, art, garden and allotment all provide welcome creative outlets in an increasingly crazy world.

Therese Lee is a screen printer and teacher: working and printing from her studio at The Hot Bed Press in Salford. Each print is multi-layered, hand drawn and hand pulled. Therese exhibits her work locally in Manchester and Cheshire and regularly runs workshops in printmaking.

Amelia Loulli is a writer who lives with her children in Cumbria. Her poetry has been shortlisted for Primers Volume 3, 2017 and the Bridport Prize 2016 & 2017. She writes when the rest of the house is sleeping, and never goes anywhere without a book.

Nico Loulli is a ten-year-old writer who lives with his mum and sisters in the Lake District, Cumbria. He is home-educated and spends many of his days building amazing things with Lego and then re-reading the Harry Potter books way past his bedtime.

Jane Lovell has been widely published in journals and anthologies. She is currently working on her first collection *This Tilting Earth*. Her pamphlet *Metastatic* is to be published in 2018 by Against the Grain Press.

Kirsten Luckins is a poet and performer based on the north-east coast. She works as a producer in the north for performance poetry organisation Apples and Snakes, and has two collections published with Burning Eye Books/Bx3. With filmmaker Laura Degnan, she runs the Celebrating Change digital storytelling project in Middlesbrough.

Thomas McColl has had poetry published in magazines such as Envoi, Iota, Prole and Ink, Sweat and Tears, and in anthologies by Hearing Eye, Eyewear and Shoestring Press. His first full collection of flash fiction and poetry, *Being With Me Will Help You Learn*, is published by Listen Softly London Press.

Andrew McMillan's debut collection *physical* was the first ever poetry collection to win The Guardian First Book Award: & also won the Fenton Aldeburgh First Collection Prize, a Somerset Maugham Award (2016), an Eric Gregory Award (2016), a Northern Writers' award (2014), and many other accolades. His second collection, *playtime* (Cape) is published in 2018. He is senior lecturer at the Manchester Writing School at MMU.

Sue Mackrell's poems and short stories have appeared in a range of publications including Agenda Poetry and Riptide Journal. She has an MA in Creative Writing and runs creative writing workshops.
http://www.writingeastmidlands.co.uk/writers-directory/sue-mackrell-2/

Sabrina Mahfouz was raised in London and Cairo. Named as a 'modern Renaissance woman' by The Scotsman, her work includes the play *Clean* (Traverse Theatre), which transferred to New York in 2014; the poetry collection *How You Might Know Me* (Out-Spoken Press); and the anthology *The Things I Would Tell You: British Muslim Women Write* (Saqi Books), which is longlisted for the Grand Prix Literary Associations Prize. www.sabrinamahfouz.com

Alwyn Marriage's ten published books include poetry, non-fiction and fiction. She is widely represented in magazines, anthologies and on-line, and gives readings all over the world. Formerly a university philosophy lecturer, Director of two international NGOs, a Rockefeller Scholar and an environmental consultant, she is currently Managing Editor of Oversteps Books and research fellow at Surrey University. www.marriages.me.uk

Roy Marshall lives in Leicestershire. His first full collection, *The Sun Bathers* (2013) was shortlisted for the Michael Murphy award. A second collection, *The Great Animator* (Shoestring Press) was published in 2017.

Mary Matusz lives in Huddersfield. Her poems have been published in anthologies and she is currently working on her first collection. She spends some of her time taming the garden next to the house and frequently re-filling the feeders for the voracious local sparrows.

Andrea Mbarushimana is a community worker, artist and writer who has been gradually losing bird-related knowledge since she was ten. You can find details of her new, short collection *The Africa in My House* at Silhouette Press. www.andrea-mbarushimana.com

Mark Mennell is a mosaic artist based in the North West who frequently references natural themes in his work, especially British garden birds, " I like to use common natural motifs in my work to dispel the myth that in some way common means uninteresting, which is anything but!"

Blue Tit, Mark Mennell

Fiona Moore lives in Greenwich. Her pamphlet *Night Letter* was shortlisted for the 2016 Michael Marks award. She was assistant editor at The Rialto for several years, blogs occasionally at Displacement and writes reviews.

Steph Morris is an artist, writer, translator and gardener, published in Rialto, In Other Words , Die Streichelwurst, and the anthology *Write to be Counted*. He holds an MA in Writing Poetry from Newcastle University/The Poetry School, and was poet in residence at Bonnington Square and House of St Barnabas with Mixed Borders, which brought poets to London gardens.

Jill Munro's first collection *Man from La Paz* was published in 2015 by Green Bottle Press. She won the Fair Acre Press Pamphlet Competition 2015 with *The Quilted Multiverse* and has been short-listed for the Bridport Prize. Jill has been awarded a Hawthornden Fellowship for 2018.

Algimantas Murza graduated college in 2003 with a diploma in editorial design; working first in a small medical publishing house then, after 4 years, for the oldest and one of the biggest Lithuanian newspapers "Lietuvos zinios". He moved to the UK in 2013. Email him for publishing work suggestions on: algis.murza@gmail.com

Kaite O'Reilly is a playwright, radio dramatist, writer, & dramaturg. She has won many awards for her work, including the 2010 Ted Hughes Award for new works in Poetry for her reworking of Aeschylus's *Persians* for National Theatre Wales in their inaugural year. She works internationally, with plays translated/produced in eleven countries worldwide. https://kaiteoreilly.com/

Lisa Osborne uses the natural environment to inspire her artwork, in particular, the coastline. She works in a variety of media - most recently using digital illustration.

Cheryl Pearson lives and writes in Manchester. Her poems have appeared in publications including The Guardian, Southword, Under The Radar, Poetry NorthWest, and The Interpreter's House. Her first full collection is *Oysterlight* (Pindrop Press, 2017).

Jeff Phelps has been publishing poetry and fiction for more than thirty years. His poetry pamphlet, *Wolverhampton Madonna* was published in 2016. He lives in Bridgnorth, Shropshire where he writes, walks and observes birds.
www.jeffphelps.co.uk

Adele Pound is a wildlife artist and keen birdwatcher based in Co Down, Northern Ireland. After graduation in England she exhibited in solo & group shows as well as using her creative skills in pub and restaurant refurbishment, hand painted furniture and crafts. She moved to Northern Ireland in 1999 where she has continued to exhibit.
https://mycreativeedge.eu/profile/adele-pound/

Black Guillemot, Adele Pound

Emma Purshouse performs her work nationally, and is a published author (writing both for adults and children) and poetry slam champion. She won the International Rubery Award for Poetry for *I Once Knew a Poem who Wore a Hat* (Fair Acre Press). She has a degree in English, an MA in creative writing, and is an experienced workshop facilitator.

Frances Rarehare is a nature photographer and artist printmaker. She is currently developing her large personally recorded collection of bird songs into a visual form as handmade books. She operates as 'Rarehare Design.'

Brenda Read-Brown has won many slams as a performance poet, but in 2018 her first book of page poetry will be published. She works with many groups such as cancer patients, people suffering from anxiety and depression, prisoners, young people and older people, and gets a lot of pleasure from helping others find their words.

Lynden Rees-Roberts has worked as an artist, musician and teacher. Since 2015 she has been running a regular monthly poetry reading programme - Poetry in Presteigne - featuring both local and guest poets from across the UK.

Susan Richardson is a poet, performer, educator and editor, whose fourth poetry collection, *Words the Turtle Taught Me*, will be published by Cinnamon Press in 2018. She is currently poet-in-residence with both the global animal welfare initiative, World Animal Day, and the British Animal Studies Network.
www.susanrichardsonwriter.co.uk

Shauna Robertson's poems have been set to music, displayed on buses, made into comic art, hung on a pub wall, and published in various lit mags and anthologies. She has two chapbooks, *Blueprints for a Minefield* (Fair Acre Press) and *Hack*. Shauna also writes for children and makes artwork.
www.shaunarobertson.wordpress.com

Andrea Robinson is a London-based artist, writer & printmaker, published in Smeuse, Extended Ley Lines and two Tate *Poetry from Art* anthologies. Her father taught her to look out for birds wherever she goes. She encountered *The long-tailed titmouse* during her Mixed Borders residency at Share Community Garden. www.andrearobinsonartist.co.uk

David Rudd-Mitchell is a Slough based 'occasional poet'. His poems have been published in magazines including BLER, Lighten Up, Zen Space and the Projectionist's Playground.

Amaal Said is a Danish-born Somali photographer and poet, currently based in London. She is a member of the Burn After Reading poetry collective and a former Barbican Young Poet. She won the Wasafiri New Writing Prize for poetry in 2015.
www.amaalsaid.com

Eileen Schaer was born in Liverpool in 1948 and now lives in the Isle of Man. She is a self taught intuitive painter acknowledged for her powerful and original poetic vision. Eileen's magical paintings depict a colourful dreamlike world. www.eileenshaer.com

Finola Scott likes writing and tickling her grandchildren. Her poems are in many places including Clear Poetry, The Lake, The Offi Pres. A Slam-winning granny - she read this year at the EIBF, as well as performing by candlelight in Rosslyn Chapel.

Derek Sellen lives in Canterbury and is publishing a collection *The Other Guernica* in 2018 with Cultured Llama Press. His poetry has been recognised in many competitions, including first prizes in Poets Meet Politics 2014, O'Bheal 2015 and Poetry Pulse 2017. Some of his work can be seen at http://www.poetrykit.org/CITN/citn%20164.htm

James Sheard's third collection *The Abandoned Settlements* (Cape) was Poetry Book Society Choice, and is shortlisted for the T.S.Eliot 2017 Prize. His pamphlet from 2003, *Hotel Mastbosch*, won the Ictus Prize, a Poetry Book Society's Pamphlet Choice. *Scattering Eva* (Cape, 2005) was shortlisted for the Forward Prize for Best First Collection & the Glen Dimplex Award for Poetry. *Dammtor* (Cape 2010) was a PBS Recommendation.

Mark Sheeky is a contemporary Renaissance Man; an oil painter, music composer, pianist, author, broadcaster, and more. His childhood passion was computer game design and programming. In 2004 he began oil painting and decided shortly after to devote his life to art.

Dorothea Smartt's poetry appears in several journals and ground-breaking anthologies, including *IC3: The Penguin Book of New Black Writing in Britain* (2000), and *A Storm Between Fingers* (Flipped Eye, 2007). Dorothea's first collection, *Connecting Medium* (2001) features a Forward Prize award winning poem. Her video/poetry installation was part of LandFall, (2009) at the Museum of London Docklands; she regularly facilitates poetry workshops.

Sue Spawn is a mixed media artist living in Malvern, inspired mainly by Nature & mostly by everything else!

Jayne Stanton lives and works in Leicestershire. She has written commissions for a county museum, University of Leicester's Centre for New Writing, and a city residency. A poetry pamphlet, *Beyond the Tune*, is published by Soundswrite Press (2014).

Peter Tinkler is an artist, illustrator, and art tutor, who teaches art classes at the mac Arts Institute, and runs his own oil painting and acrylic classes at St Paul's in the Jewellery Quarter. His work focuses primarily on the human form. His work is influenced by Goya, and classic literature and myth, among other things. His preferred medium is oil paint.

Mark Totterdell's poems have appeared widely in magazines and have occasionally won prizes. His collection *This Patter of Traces* was published by Oversteps Books in 2014. A second collection is due in 2018 from Indigo Dreams Publishing.

Rob Turner has a broad-based arts practice primarily delivering commissioned public and community art projects. He works with varied communities all over the UK, engaging participants through events and workshops to produce art in a range of media for public realm spaces.

Andrew Tyzack is a painter/printmaker and published author. He makes paintings, prints and drawings of all things natural history. House Sparrows nest in the eaves above his studio, he likes to listen to their 'song', their scuttling to and fro and their hungry nestlings.

Deborah Vass is a painter and printmaker who lives on the borders of Norfolk and Suffolk. Her artwork is inspired by the birds, plants and wildlife of her garden and the countryside of the local fens, where she sketches and records the changes in the seasons. www.deborahvass.com

Brett Westwood is a radio presenter and author, specialising in natural history. He was awarded the ZSL Thomson Reuters Award for Communicating Zoology in 2014, along with Stephen Moss, for their book and radio series *Tweet of the Day*. Since then, they have co-authored *Natural Histories* and *Wonderland*.

Lyn White lives in Kent. Her work has been published in a wide variety of journals and anthologies. She was involved in setting up and running a poetry writing project at the Hazlitt Theatre, Maidstone. Lyn is a keen birdwatcher.

Dora Williams was born in Italy, trained with several international artists and is now completing her Master degree in Fine art at the University of Gloucestershire. Her work is in private collections in the USA, Canada, Cayman Isles, Brazil, Germany, UK, Italy, Japan. www.dorawilliamsfineart.com

Katrinka Wilson is a visual artist now based in the South West. Working with drawing, painting, assemblage and words, Katrinka's work is about the magic of the ordinary and the secret wonders found in our casual encounters with the natural world.

Gordon Yapp is a printmaker, poet and illustrator. Study of nature and making detailed drawings inform his writing and printmaking. He exhibits widely, and has received many prizes including the prestigious Royal Birmingham Society of Artists' Feeney Award.

Barn Owl, Gordon Yapp

Sarah Yates is inspired by nature, planet earth, science, the cosmos, spirituality, peace... traditional crafts, modern technology, and the future. She likes to work with spraypaint, painting murals and quicker pieces on the streets, aswell as illustrations and tradional methods of painting.

Index of Poets' and Artists' Work

Acharya, Shanta 78, 81
Aird, George 28
Appleton, Rosemary 49
Archer, Richard 66
Bilston, Brian 41
Bridges, Ann 18, 84
Bromley, Carole 33
Burn, Jane 71
Byrne, Miki 79
Cockburn, Ken 19
Cole, Tina 15
Davis, Dan 66, 83, 93
Davis, Kelly 60
Doyle, Cherry 77
Elizabeth, Rhian 83
Etter, Carrie 61
Facchinetti, Giancarlo 21, 28, 46
Falkowski, Nick 57
Fowler, Heather 16
Gardiner, Tim 45
Ghassan, Aysar 82
Gibson, Gordon 58
Hardy-Dawson, Sue 46, 65, 85
Harvey, Deborah 86
Hawkins, Jen 13
Hay, Tony 49, 95
Hodson, Penny 65
Humble, Jonathan 64
Jenkins, Janet 84
Jones, Ali 47
Kielty, Paul 25, 35, 47, 68, 69, 71, 75, 79
Kingsley, Nadia 10, 18
Kinsey, Chris 54
Kurowski, Linda 67, 67
Lee, Therese 58
Loulli, Amelia 44
Loulli, Nico 45
Lovell, Jane 32
Luckins, Kirsten 14
McColl, Thomas 68
McMillan, Andrew 52
Mackrell, Sue 69
Mahfouz, Sabrina 34
Marriage, Alwyn 42, 63, 73

Marshall, Roy 22, 62
Matusz, Mary 11
Mbarushimana, Andrea 76, 80
Mennell, Mark 14, 82, 97
Moore, Fiona 31
Morris, Steph 39, 50
Munro, Jill 30
O'Reilly, Kaite 26
Osborne, Lisa 78
Pearson, Cheryl 29
Phelps, Jeff 70
Pound, Adele 3, 5, 19, 23, 38, 39, 42, 45, 54, 59, 60, 76, 77, 98
Purshouse, Emma 20
Rarehare, Frances 74, 81, 85, 86
Read-Brown, Brenda 75
Rees-Roberts, Lynden 23
Richardson, Susan 17
Robertson, Shauna 43, 87
Robinson, Andrea 25, 48, 57
Rudd-Mitchell, David 10, 45, 82
Said, Amaal 36
Schaer, Eileen 1, 53
Scott, Finola 59
Sellen, Derek 48, 91
Sheard, James 9
Sheeky, Mark 62
Smartt, Dorothea 88
Spawn, Sue 15, 72, 73
Stanton, Jayne 31
Tinkler, Peter 40
Totterdell, Mark 24, 38
Turner, Rob 56
Tyzack, Andrew 63
Vass, Deborah 12, 13, 31, 32, 33, 64, 80
White, Lyn 72
Williams, Dora 11, 30
Wilson, Katrinka 9, 37, 51
Yapp, Gordon 22, 24, 27, 70, 74, 101
Yates, Sarah 88, 89, 90

www.ingramcontent.com/pod-product-compliance
Lightning Source LLC
LaVergne TN
LVHW070332080526
838201LV00121B/409